ACCESSING INFORMATION

Beth A. Pulver and Donald C. Adcock

Heinemann Library
Chicago, Illinois

Customer Service 888-454-2279
Visit our website at www.heinemannraintree.com

Design: Richard Parker and Tinstar Design Ltd.
Photo research: Fiona Orbell and Elizabeth Alexander

Origination by Chroma Graphics (Overseas) Pte. Ltd.
Printed and bound by Leo Paper Group

ISBN: 978-1-4329-1227-7 (hc)

13 12 11 10 09
10 9 8 7 6 5 4 3 2 1

Library of Congress Cataloging-in-Publication Data
Pulver, Beth A.
  Accessing information / Beth A. Pulver and Donald C. Adcock.
     p. cm. -- (Information literacy skills)
  Includes bibliographical references and index.
  ISBN 978-1-4329-1227-7
  1. Research--Methodology--Juvenile literature. 2. Information retrieval--Juvenile literature. 3. Reference sources--Juvenile literature. 4. Information literacy--Juvenile literature. I. Adcock, Donald C. II. Title.
  ZA3080.P852 2008
  025.5'24--dc22
                          2008018775

Acknowledgments
The author and publishers are grateful to the following for permission to reproduce copyright material: © 1994–2001 David K. Brown. All rights reserved. p. **26**; © 2006 TopFoto/Jon Mitchell p. **15**; © Alamy pp. /Dennis Hallinan **40**, /Ian Shaw **8**, /Julie Mowbray **31**, /Jupiterimages/Brand X **7**, /Jupiterimages/Creatas **5**, /Krebs Hanns **9**, /Photodisc **36**, /Vstock **29**; © Corbis pp. /Gabe Palmer **4**, /image100 **13**, /John Hicks **20**, /LWA-Sharie Kennedy **38**, /Pfütze/zefa **43**, /Rick Gomez **33**; © Getty Images pp. /Eightfish **6**, /Nick White **30**; © iStockphoto/Jennifer Sheets p. **22**; © PhotoDisc/StockTrek p. **11**; © The British Library p. **25**; © The New York Public Library p. **25**; © The Statue of Liberty—Ellis Island Foundation, Inc. p. **24**.

Background features and cover photograph reproduced with permission of © iStockphoto.

Every effort has been made to contact copyright holders of any material reproduced in this book. Any omissions will be rectified in subsequent printings if notice is given to the publishers.

Contents

 Some words are shown in bold, **like this.** You can find the definitions for these words in the glossary.

Identifying the Need for Information

You may not realize it, but you are constantly accessing and evaluating information. If your friend tells you the latest news, that's information. If your mother reminds you of a doctor's appointment, that's information. When you read a school book, watch TV, read the newspaper, or surf the Web, you are getting information.

Sometimes you need information on a specific topic. You may need information to help you answer a specific question. When you carefully look for information to help answer a question, it is known as **research**. Research is not just for answering a question for school. Good research skills will help you throughout your life.

This book will discuss how to identify the need for information to answer a specific question, and it will offer help in determining how much information is needed. It will provide strategies for narrowing or broadening a topic in order to find the necessary information. This book will also help you with strategies for finding information and identifying a variety of resources you might use in conducting research.

The librarian is one of the best research tools you have available.

Librarians

If you have a big research project, or even a complicated question you want answered, knowing where to look for answers can seem overwhelming. One of the best places to start is the library. Libraries have access to much more information than you do by yourself.

One of the best people to help you start your research project is a librarian. People go to school for a long time to become a librarian. After high school and college, a librarian also needs to get a master's degree. Librarians learn about different research techniques and resources. A librarian might not be an expert on your subject, but he or she will be an expert in helping you research your subject.

People used to imagine piles of books when they thought of research. Some research still requires many books, but people now often turn to the Internet and other electronic resources as their first stop for information. Librarians can help with your electronic searches for information, too.

Ask a question

Sometimes the best way to start a research project is to ask a question. A question will help guide you in finding the information you need. Some people refer to this question as a research question, or a problem statement.

For some questions, you will just need a one-word or one-sentence answer. Complicated questions or assignments may require looking at many different magazines, books, or journals. You may want to use the **Internet** or other **electronic sources**, like online **databases**, to locate the information needed to answer your questions or provide solutions to your problems. The more complex the question or problem, the more sources you are likely to need to examine in order to find an answer or solution.

What is a library?

There are many different kinds of libraries. A school library usually contains books at the right reading level for the students at the school. Your school library probably has fiction as well as nonfiction. Your library may also have computers and other resources. Usually, only students at the school are allowed to use the school library or borrow books from it.

School libraries can be very different from each other. Some schools may have a library media center with many types of resources, and others may have a small room with only a few books.

If you aren't used to working in a library, finding your way around can be difficult.

Public libraries

A public library is usually run by a town or city. Most towns think it is important that their residents have access to information. Everyone is welcome at a public library, but usually only residents of the city or nearby cities can borrow books. Sometimes only residents of the city or nearby cities can use library resources like computers. A public library may have a wide variety of fiction and nonfiction books, DVDs, CDs, and magazines. Some of these materials will be appropriate for you, but others will be too complicated or adult for your needs.

Some public libraries may have a special children's area with comfortable chairs, and even toys. Public libraries usually carry government information, such as tax forms, or information about special programs the government provides. Many public libraries have special programs, such as book readings or town meetings. Public libraries have all these resources because they exist to provide services to the residents of the town.

College and university libraries

Colleges and universities have very large libraries with thousands and thousands of books. They also have large collections of journals related to the courses taught at the college. Libraries at colleges and universities provide resources and assistance to the students and professors who are conducting research. They may have a small collection of fiction books to read for pleasure, but the literature collection is for research purposes. Many college and university libraries allow anyone to use their resources in the library, but only allow their students and teachers to borrow things from it.

Special libraries

Museums, hospitals, and businesses can all have libraries attached to them. These are known as special libraries. In a regular library you can wander around looking at different books, but in many special libraries you have to ask the librarian for the book you want, and he or she brings it to you. These special libraries often have very valuable books that they need to keep safe for future research.

Whichever kind of library you are using, the best way to find what you need is to start with a librarian.

Forming questions

Let's look at some examples of how to form research questions.

A group of students is studying the periodic table of elements. Each student has been assigned an element to research. The student must find the atomic number, the number of protons, and the number of electrons for the element. The student must also find the melting or boiling point for the element.

Before beginning the research, the students form their assignments into a series of questions:

- What is the atomic number for the element gold?
- What is the number of protons in the element gold?
- What is the melting point for the element gold?

Now the student knows what to look for, and can decide the best place to find the answers.

Research can be very fulfilling, but before you can answer the question, you need to know what question to ask.

The problem-solving process

Research involves a sequence of steps to answer questions or solve problems:

- Determine the problem
- Create a research question
- Identify what you know now
- Identify what you still need to find out
- Identify possible resources
- Create possible solutions
- Evaluate the solutions
- Present your solution

Here is another example. Two boys wondered how their hockey skate blades allowed them to move across the ice so easily. They first put this thought into a question: "How do hockey skate blades work on ice?" The boys decided what they already know about skates and the blades on the skates. They now know what they need to find out in order to answer their question. Now they can go to the library and begin their search for possible resources. They may have to create more questions as more information is found. As they read they find information to generate possible answers. They evaluate the information and decide on the best possible answer.

Research questions for "How do hockey skate blades work on ice?"

- What happens when an ice skate blade moves across the ice?
- What affects the speed of the skater?
- What scientific knowledge or principles apply to this question?
- How are hockey skate blades different from the blades of other types of ice skates?

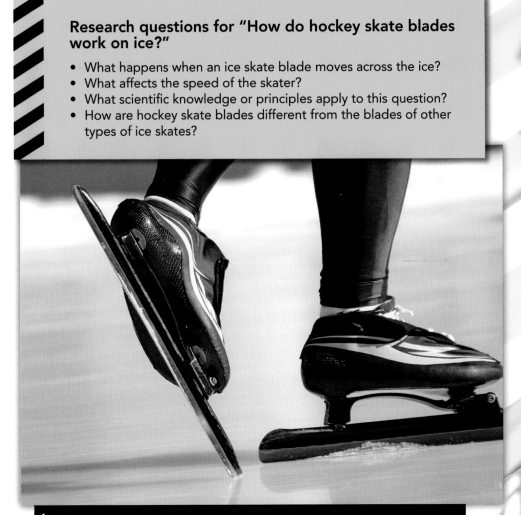

It is obvious that ice skates can help a person glide more quickly over the ice. But how do they do that? Having good questions is the important starting point for any research.

Answering Big Questions

The students researching the elements had fairly straightforward questions. Some questions are more complicated.

Imagine a group of students studying constellations. They have learned that the constellations seen in the eastern skies during the summer months are not the ones they will see in the same skies in the winter months. They need to find out why they are not the same. Before they can begin looking for the information, the students need to create a research question. The research question for this topic might be "Why do the constellations change locations in the sky from one season to the next?"

Since the students have been studying the solar system in their science class, they already know some information about constellations. Now they decide what it is they still need to know about constellations in order to answer the question. Once they know what information they need, they can begin to identify sources and gather information they will use to find answers. The students will then create and analyze possible solutions to the question and present the best solution to their class.

A matter of opinion

We all have certain opinions. Some opinions are what is known as a matter of taste, such as your favorite color or a food you don't like. It's almost impossible to argue about these things. You may think chocolate is the best flavor of ice cream, and your father thinks it's vanilla. There's probably nothing you can say to change his opinion.

You do not need any information or research to support these kinds of opinions. There are other opinions, however, that should be based in research. Who is the best candidate for political office? Where is the best place to shop for groceries? The answers to these questions need to be based in research.

Well-researched opinions

Students aren't the only people who need to do research. Adults who need to present arguments or opinions also need to do research to make sure their opinions are valid. Many people dislike reading opinions or information with which they disagree. This is understandable. However, people who want to be taken seriously, not just in research but also in life, must learn to see others' points of view. If you keep an open mind, you can learn a lot from others' opinions. You may change your mind on some issues, or you may come to feel more strongly about your own opinion.

When asking questions, you must first have a workable topic. Some subjects, like the solar system, are too big to handle in one question.

Case study: Should smoking in public be banned?

Many cities, towns, and states have laws that ban smoking in public places. What if a government was trying to decide whether or not such a law would be a good idea for its town?

In order to answer the question "Should smoking be banned in public places?," the lawmakers must identify what information is needed. The lawmakers should form questions based on what they already know on the topic and what they need to know. Below are some questions they might start with.

Should smoking be banned in public places?

- What are the issues surrounding the question?
- What countries, cities, or states currently have bans on smoking, and what were the results of those bans?
- How would the ban affect businesses that currently allow smoking?
- What is secondhand smoke?
- What are the effects of secondhand smoke?
- What is the definition of a "public place"?
- Is there a difference between public places that are enclosed and public places in the open?

These questions will help lawmakers decide what sources of information will provide the answers to the questions. These resources will include books, websites, or interviews with experts. After they've completed this research, the lawmakers can then analyze their information to create a possible solution and prepare the arguments to support their solution.

Even if two people carefully research a question such as "Should smoking be banned in public places?," they may still come up with different answers. One person may think the health issues are the most important, and so she supports the ban. Another person may believe economic issues are more important. He may worry that banning smoking means restaurants will go out of business. He does not support the ban.

If these two people want to have a discussion about the issue, they should make sure their research is thorough, and that they listen to each other respectfully.

Rules for discussing opinions

- Make sure you've done your research.
- Make sure you understand all the issues, not just the ones you care about.
- Don't bring in information that isn't relevant.
- Fight fair, don't make personal attacks.
- Listen to the other person's point of view.

Should smoking be banned in places like restaurants?

Narrowing or Broadening the Topic

When you have a research question to be answered or problem to be solved, you usually already know some facts about the topic. If you've been studying the topic in school or have a special interest in it, you may know quite a bit about it. Figuring out what you already know can help you develop your research question. A **KWL chart** is a way of organizing this information. K stands for Know, W stands for Want to know, and L stands for what you Learn in your research. The first two columns are filled in before your research starts, and the last is filled in as you work.

KWL chart

Topic: Smoking bans

Question: Should smoking be banned in public places?

What I <u>K</u>now	What I <u>W</u>ant to know	What I <u>L</u>earned
Secondhand smoke is unhealthy	Where has smoking in public places already been banned?	Public places include parks, beaches, and sidewalks.
Public places include restaurants and stores	What are the economic issues?	The majority of people approve of bans on smoking.
		Many business people do not agree with the bans.

Narrowing the topic

Once you have determined what it is you need to know, the next step is to either narrow or broaden the topic. Some teachers assign very broad research topics. This is usually done so that each student can narrow the topic down to something that is of interest to him or her. Imagine a teacher assigned "World War II" as a topic. Obviously this is a large topic. You might narrow it to a specific battle. Another student might want to research the causes of World War II.

Sometimes it can feel like the Battle of the Bulge refers to too much information! Narrowing your topic makes research and writing easier.

If your topic is too broad, you become overwhelmed by the amount of information you find. This is especially true when using the Internet. If you enter "World War II" into Google or another **search engine**, you will get over 100,000,000 **hits**. When you use a search engine, the engine finds any website that mentions the word or phrase you typed. So a search on World War II may include useful historical information, but it may also include a site that only mentions the phrase once. Even using a specific term, such as "Battle of the Bulge," a famous World War II battle, will yield a lot of hits. However, the more specific a term you start with, the easier it will be to decide which sites are useful. Make sure you are using the correct term, and include as much information as needed. If you search for "Battle Bulge," you may wind up getting diet tips. However, if you search for "Battle Bulge World War II," you are more likely to only get information you want.

There are many techniques you can use to help narrow your topic down to something manageable.

Narrowing a broad topic to a more specific one makes the research and writing much easier. If you are having trouble narrowing your topic, you will need to determine **key words** related to your topic. There are several sources you can use to find key words.

You can type in your subject into a library's **online catalog**, and it will display related topics that may help narrow your topic. Another place to look would be the **table of contents** or **index** of books on your topic. You might even read an article in a general **encyclopedia** on your topic, looking for more specific topics. You can also search an online database, Internet search engine, or **directory** in the same way you searched the online catalog for related topics.

Thinking of a triangle may help you see how you can narrow your topic. Draw an upside-down triangle, as seen below. Using the terms you found in your research, you can begin to fill in the narrowing triangle. As you fill in the triangle, you will stop when you have found a topic that is of interest to you and has enough information available to answer your question or solve your problem.

Narrowing a topic from broad to specific

16

Broadening the topic

Some topics might be too narrow instead of too broad. An example of a narrow topic would be "Why do birds lay eggs of different colors?" The answer to this question is fairly easy to find—birds lay eggs of different colors to protect the eggs. However, this does not give you enough information for a research paper. You may want to broaden this topic to "How do animals use coloration for protection?" If your topic is too narrow, you may become frustrated because you cannot find, or easily find, enough information to answer your question.

Imagine a student decides to research gargoyles. Gargoyles are a type of decoration found on the upper parts of medieval buildings. This topic is so narrow that there is not enough to help the student create a question. The student can use some of the same resources used for narrowing a topic to broaden it.

Just as an inverted, or upside-down, triangle helped to widen a topic, a regular triangle can help you visualize, or see, the broadening of your topic. If you are using a broadening triangle, you must also make sure to find a topic that is of interest to you. You will need to make sure that there is enough information available to answer the question or solve the problem.

A triangle chart can help expand the topic from gargoyles to medieval architecture.

Widening a topic from specific to broad

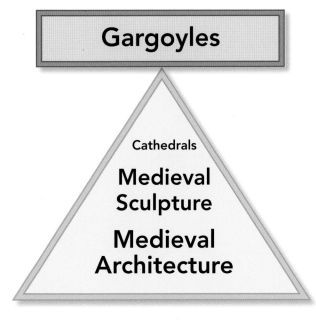

Strategies for Locating Information

As we've seen, there are many different kinds of questions. Some questions can be answered with a sentence, still others need a paper or book. The students searching for the facts related to elements only needed a short answer to their questions. On the other hand, the hockey skate question the two boys had asks about how something works. This question may require reading a paragraph or two to find the answer, and may require more than one source. Forming an opinion on smoking bans requires reading materials on all sorts of subjects. The more difficult the question or problem, the more sources you will need to use to find the answers or solutions.

Guide for locating information

Is the answer a sentence?
These are the types of questions that require only a sentence or two from a source to answer.

Example: What year did Christopher Columbus land in the Americas?

Is the answer a paragraph?
These types of questions or problems require a paragraph or two from a source to answer or solve.

Example: How does the process of photosynthesis work?

Is the answer in books?
These are types of questions that require reading many paragraphs to answer. These paragraphs would be found in a book or books.

Example: How are Ares, the Greek god of war, and Mars, the Roman god of war, similar?

Using a table of contents

There are sections within a source that help you locate information about your topic. One section is the table of contents. The table of contents is a list of the titles of chapters or sections of a book arranged in the order in which they appear in the book.

Looking at each chapter title in the table of contents can help you determine how much information, if any, the source will provide to answer your question. Some tables of contents may have subheadings listed under the chapter title. They may be indented or in a different type of font to show that they are a part of the chapter. These subheadings provide additional details on the information found in the resource.

The table of contents will also show other places within the book where information might be found on the topic. They could include a timeline, a **glossary**, an index, and a list of other sources where you might find information on your topic.

Table of Contents

The table of contents in a book helps you determine the content of a book, and whether the book will provide information you need.

Using an index

Remember the student researching gargoyles? Imagine the student's library search turns up a book on French architecture. The book is over 600 pages long! There isn't enough time to read the entire book, but the student still needs the information. One thing the student can do is look at the index. The index is usually the last section in the book. It is an alphabetical list of terms, names, and subjects found in the book. Next to each term or name is a list of page numbers where you can find information on those terms or names.

Some indexes list pictures, graphs, and charts found in the book in a different way. For example they might use italics, such as *this*. Some indexes may have subheadings listed under the term, name, or subject. They may be indented, or a different type of print, to show that they are a part of the term, name, or subject. In our example, under "churches," you might find a subhead of "gargoyles." This would tell you that there is information on gargoyles that are found on churches.

Without an index, going through a book to find one piece of information would be like looking for a needle in a haystack.

Index

An index gives you specific pages where information can be found within a book.

Using a glossary

Many books have pages in them that look like a research source you've been using ever since you started school, a **dictionary**. This section in a book that is similar to a dictionary is called a glossary. Dictionaries give you more information about a word than a glossary does. A dictionary will tell you whether the word is a noun, verb, adverb, or adjective. It may also tell you what language the word comes from and an example of how the word is used in a sentence.

A glossary defines the word and may also show how the word is pronounced. The glossary defines the word only as it relates to the topic of the book. For example, in a book about Africa the glossary definition of a desert would probably say, "place that receives very little rain." If you were to look in a dictionary, you would find other definitions of desert, such as, "place in the ocean where there is no life." Because the information listed in a glossary is more specific to your topic, there are some cases where a glossary can be more helpful than a dictionary.

The words and definitions in a glossary are related to the special content of a book.

Mendel's Laws	principles of heredity established in the 19th century by Gregor Mendel
methodology	using a particular method or set of rules when doing something, for example, scientific methodology
moderator	someone who presides over an event and makes sure the rules are followed
mutation	error in the replication, or copying, of DNA that produces a change in the development of an organism. Mutations can improve a living organism, damage it, or even kill it.
refutation	challenging an argument using reasoning and evidence
trait	characteristic or feature that is passed on from parent to offspring

Skimming and scanning

Do you wonder how librarians can help you find so much information? After all, even a librarian doesn't have time to read every book. There are techniques that librarians use when they are helping you locate information. They may use a technique called **skimming**. Skimming is used when you first look at a resource in the research process and are trying to determine if it contains information about your topic. When you skim an article or large amount of text, you are reading titles, subheadings, illustrations, or even the first and last sentences of a paragraph, to see if the information you are looking for may be found in this source. You may even read the first and last paragraphs of sections to find summaries of the content. You will quickly read paragraphs looking for the main ideas or supporting details. After skimming you will decide if the source is one you will look at later for more detailed information.

See if you can skim the following encyclopedia entry to find the important information:

Gargoyle

The Gothic gargoyle was usually a grotesque bird or animal sitting on the back of a cornice and projecting forward for several feet in order to throw the water far from the building. The term is often loosely applied to any grotesque or fantastic beast, such as the *chimères* (chimeras) that decorate the parapets of Notre-Dame de Paris.

Taken from the Encyclopedia Britannica, *online edition*

Skimming an article or book is like skimming water—you touch the surface but do not go very deep.

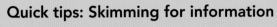

Quick tips: Skimming for information

- Read the title.
- Read the introduction or first paragraph.
- Read the first sentence of every other paragraph.
- Read any headings or subheadings.
- Notice any pictures, charts, or graphs.
- Notice any words that are italic or bold.
- Read the summary or last paragraph.

Scanning for information

Another technique is called **scanning**. Scanning is a good technique to use for locating specific information, such as names, dates, and locations of places. It is also used for reviewing graphs, charts, and tables. Scanning is used more for locating specific information you can use in answering your question. As you quickly read down the page, you are looking for key words. Sometimes these are in bold type or in phrases. When you scan, in most cases you already know what you are looking for. The techniques of skimming and scanning work best when using books, magazines, or newspapers, rather than a computer screen.

Quick tips: Scanning for information

- State the specific information you are looking for in the form of a question.
- Predict how the answer will appear and what clues you might use to only find that answer.
- Use headings, bold or italic print, and graphics to identify sections where information might be found.
- Selectively read and skip through sections of text.

Using databases

A database is a collection of records stored on a computer or computer system. If you were trying to find information about a family member who immigrated to the United States, you might visit the website www.ellisisland.org. This organization has put all of the records of people who entered this country through Ellis Island into a database. You can search this database from your personal computer.

This is one example of
a searchable database.

A subject search on a library's catalog will provide a list of source titles available in the library. You will use the titles to decide if it is a source you want to look at further.

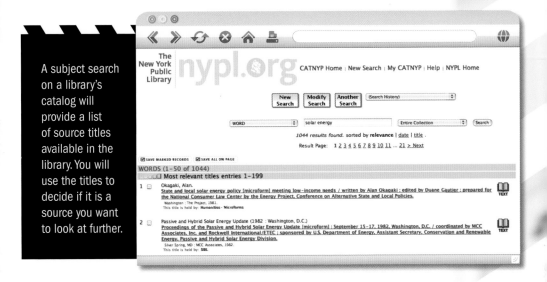

Most libraries have their catalogs stored in online databases. Other databases may contain years of magazines or journals. You could search ten years of a magazine by entering one or two terms into a database.

The secret to a successful database search is to use key words. Key words are significant words taken from your research question. If a student's research question is "What are the natural resources of Germany?," the key words for this search would be "Germany" and "natural resources."

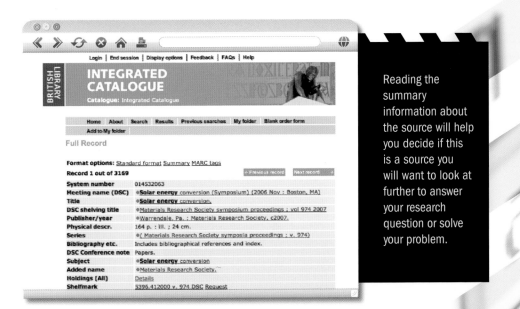

Reading the summary information about the source will help you decide if this is a source you will want to look at further to answer your research question or solve your problem.

Internet searching

A large amount of information is available on the Internet. In order to use that **online** information, you must have a computer with access to the Internet. Most public and school libraries have computers available. Information can be found by using either a directory or a search engine.

Directories

An Internet directory is a collection of websites, but it does not contain all websites. Directories may choose websites based on an expert's opinion of the content. Or directories may feature websites that pay to be included. A directory is sort of like a phone book. A phone book is a good place to find a lot of information, but not everyone is listed in the book.

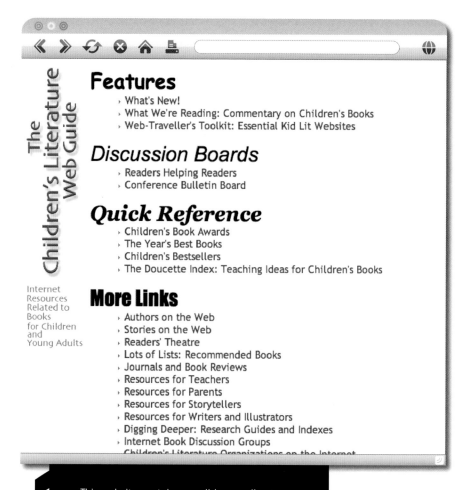

The Children's Literature Web Guide

Internet Resources Related to Books for Children and Young Adults

Features
› What's New!
› What We're Reading: Commentary on Children's Books
› Web-Traveller's Toolkit: Essential Kid Lit Websites

Discussion Boards
› Readers Helping Readers
› Conference Bulletin Board

Quick Reference
› Children's Book Awards
› The Year's Best Books
› Children's Bestsellers
› The Doucette Index: Teaching Ideas for Children's Books

More Links
› Authors on the Web
› Stories on the Web
› Readers' Theatre
› Lots of Lists: Recommended Books
› Journals and Book Reviews
› Resources for Teachers
› Resources for Parents
› Resources for Storytellers
› Resources for Writers and Illustrators
› Digging Deeper: Research Guides and Indexes
› Internet Book Discussion Groups
Children's Literature Organizations on the Internet

This website contains a well-known directory of websites about children's literature.

With a directory, you do not have access to the millions of websites that are not included in the directory. When you are beginning to gather information to answer your research question or solve your problem, a directory is a good beginning point because you can browse for ideas, search for general concepts, or get a feel for what is available on the topic.

Quick tips: Searching

Use quotation marks when searching for phrases or groups of words, for example:
- "history hula hoops"
- "rio de janeiro"

Do not include words such as "the," "and," or "of."

Search engines

Search engines are helpful when using unique key words or searching for very focused topics. A search engine uses your key words to search the entire Internet. If you use a search engine when beginning your research, your key words may provide you with hundreds of thousands of websites, many of which will not provide you the information you need to answer your question or solve your problem. It is very important when using a search engine that your key words are very specific to your topic. This will help to narrow the number of websites you will find.

Fees

Some websites and databases may charge fees. For example, sites that let you look up personal information about people often cost money. Before you use such a site, you may want to talk to your librarian. Your library may already have a subscription to the site, letting you use it for free. Usually these sources are also available for you to use at home with permission from the library. The librarian will be able to give you the information you will need to use the sources at home. The librarian may also know of another free resource.

Remember, you should never use a credit card online without first discussing the site with a trusted adult.

Web pages: Keeping track

After you have conducted your Web search using either a directory or a search engine, you will have a list of websites on the screen. You will look at the titles and basic summaries to decide if this is a website that will help you.

The **URL**, or Web address, may also determine if it is a website you will want to use. The URL is divided into three parts:
- The first part tells you that it is an address on the World Wide Web with the letters www.
- The next part of the address is the name of the Web page. Remember, website names can be misleading.
- The final part is the domain name.

The domain name tells where the Web page is registered. The most common domain names are companies, educational institutions, organizations, and governments. The last three are the most reliable types of sites. Sometimes a "/" will follow the domain name. This means that you are on a page of a larger website. You will want to copy down the URL, or Web address, to find the article later for further research.

Quick tips: Domain names

You can get clues to the types of websites you find from the domain names.
- .com = commercial site
- .gov = governmental site
- .org = organization (noncommercial)
- .edu = school or university
- .mil = U.S. military site
- .net = network service provider, Internet administrative site

International sites

Sites based in other countries often have two letters after the name of the site. For example, in "www.ucalgary.ca/," the "ca" indicates that the site is based in Canada. Some common abbreviations are:

ca	Canada
cn	China
jp	Japan
uk	United Kingdom

Using a computer can seem like a private act, but don't be lured into a false sense of safety or security.

Safety

The Internet can be an exciting place. You have the freedom to go anywhere in the world. You can meet exciting people you would never have access to in your hometown. You can go shopping or do research at any time of day or night, in your pajamas or in your clothes.

All of this freedom and excitement, however, comes with certain responsibilities and concerns. There are two main types of Internet safety concerns.

The first is fraud, or theft. You would never give your parents' credit card to a stranger, but when you buy something online you may be doing just that. You should always make sure your parents look at a website and determine that it is safe before buying something. Never give out personal information, such as your social security number or bank account, in answer to an e-mail.

The other safety concern is for your personal safety. You can pretend to be anyone you want online. That means that other people may be pretending as well. Never tell anyone you meet online your address or phone number. It's best to make sure you only "chat" in rooms that have moderators.

A Variety of Sources

Good researchers use a variety of sources to get their information. Using a variety of sources is important because it allows the researchers to verify the information they are finding in more than one place. Using more than one source may also provide different points of view on a topic.

As you begin to locate information to answer your question or solve your problem, you will find that different sources provide different types of information. The question to be answered or problem to be solved will determine whether you will begin your search for information using print or electronic resources.

It is important to have a good balance of electronic and print resources when conducting research. For this researcher, good physical balance is also important!

Reference books

Beginning researchers often start their research with books found in the reference section of the library. These books cannot usually be checked out of the library. As mentioned earlier, different questions require different amounts of information to answer. There are times when you may need a dictionary to answer a question because it gives the definition, pronunciation, or spelling of a word. Sometimes the question requires more information, so the best source might be an encyclopedia because it contains more detailed information.

Encyclopedias provide an overview on a topic.

Encyclopedias

Encyclopedia articles provide a general overview of a topic. Encyclopedias are best used when you need to find specific facts on a subject or need some general knowledge on a subject. They are a good resource to use when you are just beginning your research, because they will provide needed background information on a wide variety of subjects. Information in the encyclopedia is arranged alphabetically. There are two types of encyclopedias, general and subject specific. General encyclopedias are usually in large sets and contain information on a wide range of subjects. Subject-specific encyclopedias only contain information on a single subject, like world history, chemistry, or animals. These types of encyclopedias may be a single book or a multiple-book set. Encyclopedias are available in print, online, or on compact disc. Online, compact disc, and print versions of the same encyclopedia may differ from one another.

Dictionaries

Dictionaries are arranged alphabetically and are generally used to find definitions of words, verify spellings, find the origin of a word, show how a word is pronounced, or even find a synonym for the word. There may also be a section at the end of the dictionary that will have biographical and geographical names. Dictionaries are available in print and online. Like encyclopedias, there are different types of dictionaries.

Special dictionaries

There are special dictionaries on subjects such as history, people, and places. These special dictionaries, like the ones used for words, provide brief entries with facts specific to that subject.

Historical dictionaries, for example, provide entries on different historical events, people in history, and places where historical events took place. Biographical dictionaries provide facts on people. A biographical dictionary will give a person's name, birth and death dates, nationality, occupation, and a brief description of the person's life. Geographical dictionaries provide facts about places. They will give the pronunciation of a place; tell whether it is a city, country, or type of geographical formation; and give its location. The entries in these dictionaries are arranged alphabetically. Most dictionaries are found in a single volume, but some dictionaries on specific subjects could be in several volumes.

[Main Entry] **sum·ma·ry**
[Pronunciation] \se – me – r *also* sem-r ? *or* mer-
[Part of Speech] *adjective*
[Etymology or Word Origin] Middle English, from Medieval Latin *summarius*, from Latin *summa* sum
[Date] 15th century
[Definitions] **1:comprehensive**; *especially* :covering the main points succinctly. **2 a:**done without delay or formality :quickly executed <a *summary* dismissal> **b:**of, relating to, or using a summary proceeding <a *summary* trial>

synonyms see **concise**

The *Oxford English Dictionary*, or OED, is considered the most complete dictionary of the English language. It contains words used in all English-speaking countries. The OED is an excellent research tool. It lists not only current definitions of words, but old ones as well. The example on the left shows the features of a typical dictionary entry.

A thesaurus is a special kind of dictionary used for finding synonyms of words. Thesauruses are used more for writing than for research.

Atlases and almanacs

Atlases are books of maps. They may contain maps showing the boundaries of countries; their geographical features, such as mountains, rivers, and lakes; and the types of climate of those countries. Atlases can have current maps of the world, or they can have maps from different times in history.

Almanacs are published every year and contain bits of information on a wide variety of subjects, such as people, weather for the year, flags of the countries of the world, and statistics about those countries. With so much information, the best way to find what you are looking for is to use the index, which is often found at the front in an almanac.

An atlas can be a good source of information. The maps show information in a visual form.

Finding books

Nonfiction books are written on a wide range of topics. These books are arranged in the library by a number that relates to the subject of the book. Books can best be located by using the online or card catalog in the library. Information may be found in the online catalog by searching using the name of the author, the title of the work, the subject, or key words you might be looking for.

Most school and public libraries arrange their nonfiction books according to the **Dewey decimal system**. This system assigns a number to every kind of book. For example, if you are looking for a book about religion, it will be assigned a number that starts with the numeral 2. If you are looking for a book about science, its number will start with the numeral 5. If you learn the basics of the Dewey decimal system, it will save you time in almost any library.

The basics of the Dewey decimal system

- 000 – Computer science, information, and general works
- 100 – Philosophy and psychology
- 200 – Religion
- 300 – Social sciences
- 400 – Language
- 500 – Science
- 600 – Technology
- 700 – Arts and recreation
- 800 – Literature
- 900 – History and geography

Periodicals

Periodicals, which include magazines, journals, and newspapers, provide current information on a variety of topics. Journals are considered to be more educational than magazines. Newspapers provide immediate information or facts about events. Periodicals can be found online in what is called "full text." Some periodicals are available on the Internet, while others require the use of a database for access. Some newspapers can be accessed on the Internet daily.

Databases

Databases are computer resources. They are usually accessed by using a computer connected to the Internet. Libraries and schools pay a fee to have the right to use the information on the database. There are as many different kinds of databases as there are books and periodicals. Databases include information from encyclopedias, articles from magazines and newspapers, and reference sources. The library will have a list of the databases they subscribe to. Databases are easier to keep current because they are electronic. Finding information in a database is similar to searching for information on the Internet. The information you find may be text from books, magazines, journals, and newspapers. You may also find pictures, graphs, and tables.

SNOWBOARDING: outdoor sports and games 796.6

Masoff, Joy
    Extreme sports: snowboard! By Joy Masoff
    Washington, D.C., National Geographic Books, 2002

64 pp., illus.

Sports – Snowboarding   2. Outdoor sports and games

I. Title

RC1220.S55   796.6

Most libraries have switched from physical card catalogs to an electronic version, but you might need to use a card index. These two cards show a subject index card for snowboarding, and what a book entry card would look like.

Primary sources

Researchers generally talk about two kinds of sources, primary and secondary. **Primary sources** are historical documents—things written, made, or used by people in history. Secondary sources are things written about people or events in history, or written about primary sources.

Abraham Lincoln's diary is a primary source. A book about Lincoln's diary is a secondary source. Primary sources are original records, **memoirs**, and oral histories. Documents could include letters, diaries, journals, speeches, interviews, photographs, or government papers. These documents provide the resources necessary for historical research.

One day even your personal journal could be used as a primary source.

Memoirs

A memoir is similar to a diary. In a diary a person might write down a variety of things that happened. For example, you might write about what you had for breakfast, a fight you had with a friend, and maybe also current events in the world. A memoir is generally written by someone after an event is over. A president might look at his diaries from his time in office, and from those diaries make a memoir about an important time period. A memoir will generally only include information that is important to a specific event or time period. It will not usually include personal information.

Personal interviews

Personal interviews are often used to get an individual's reflections or opinion on an event, period of time, piece of literature, etc. These are excellent sources of information that may not be found in any type of print or online source. Many history museums and libraries keep collections of such interviews. When doing research, you may want to conduct an interview yourself.

Writing interview questions

- Create a list of key words about the topic.
- Use each key word to write a question to learn about the topic.
- Create enough questions to have enough information.
- Questions should be clearly stated.
- Questions should allow for a variety of answers.
- Questions should require more than a "yes" or "no" answer.
- Questions should encourage sharing of memories.
- Remember, interview questions are just a starting point. Remain flexible and listen to your subject—you never know where he or she might take you.

Television

Are you looking for a good excuse to watch TV? You can consider it research! You may find documentaries, or even regular TV shows, that provide excellent information. For example, if you are researching teens and diets, you may find a talk show about that subject. Many news and talk shows allow you to order **transcripts** of programs. A transcript is a written recording of everything that happened on the show. It would be hard to watch a TV show while taking accurate notes, so you should plan on recording the program or getting a transcript. To get a transcript, you can view the directions after the show or look at the show's website for directions. Many databases contain transcripts in their records.

TV shows are good for relaxing, but some can also be used for research.

DVDs and videos

Today, you can find DVDs and TV shows about subjects ranging from endangered animals to Roman history. You can use your library's catalog to search for DVDs and recordings of shows the same way you use it to search for books, magazines, and journals. If you know of a TV show that frequently discusses a topic you are interested in, you might check the website for that show as well. Many shows will list past episodes online. Some of these shows can even be viewed over your computer.

Just like with print and electronic resources, you will have to find a way to **cite** video resources. The details for citing videos and TV shows are different than for citing print resources, but the idea is the same. Make sure to discuss citations with your teacher.

Sources of information	When to use them	What to watch out for
Encyclopedias - General - Subject specific	Use for facts or general knowledge on a subject.	Check the date for currency.
Dictionaries	Use for definitions or facts on a subject.	Check the date—new words are added regularly. Check the intended audience. Some may not have as many definitions as others.
Atlases	Use when looking for geographical information.	Check the date for currency.
Nonfiction books	Use for facts and general or detailed knowledge on a subject.	Who is the author? Check the publication date.
Periodicals - Newspapers - Journals - Magazines	Use for information on current topics.	Check for currency and bias of information.
Databases	Use these on a computer for information on current topics.	Check for currency and bias of information.
Internet - Directories - Websites	Use this world-wide collection of information on a computer for finding more sources or comparing products and sources.	Check for currency, bias, and inaccurate information.
Personal interviews	Use for individual reflections or opinions.	Questions should provide answers needed. Questions should allow for expanded answers. Memories are not always accurate.
Educational videos, computer programs, television programs - CD-ROMs - DVDs/Videos	Use for facts on a subject, general knowledge on a subject, or more detailed information.	Check for currency, bias, and inaccurate information.

Plagiarism

When you have found all of your sources and done all of your research, you will begin writing your paper. One thing you must be careful to avoid is **plagiarism**. Plagiarism is another word for cheating by copying. When you commit plagiarism, you submit someone else's ideas or words as your own.

Many people do this accidentally. They copy phrases or sentences from a book or article, forget where they found the work, and put it in their own paper. Other people believe, incorrectly, that if they have changed the words around, they have not committed plagiarism.

You wouldn't steal someone's things or answers on a test, so why would you steal their thoughts?

Catching plagiarism

Your teacher has many ways of discovering if you have copied your paper. If your work does not seem like it was written by you, your teacher will probably become suspicious. If you have copied from another student, past or present, the teacher may recognize the work or may ask other teachers if they recognize it. If you copy from a published source or something you find online, your teacher may type a few sentences into a search engine and discover that you have copied the work. Today, teachers can choose from several free software options for help in finding plagiarism.

Most schools have codes of conduct with rules against plagiarizing. The penalties may include you failing the assignment or even the class. In some schools and colleges, you may be expelled, or kicked out, of school for plagiarizing, even if you do so accidentally. Adults have lost their jobs and the respect of other people for committing plagiarism.

How to avoid plagiarizing

Take careful notes:
- Make sure you take notes as you read. Write down where you read something and what page it was on.
- If you copy a quotation from a book, make sure to mark it as a quotation.

Give credit where credit is due:
- If you agree with something you read in a book, you can use a phrase such as "As Jane Austen says. . . ." This lets the reader know whose idea the thought is.
- When writing your bibliography and footnotes, include more than is strictly necessary.

Use quotation marks:
- If you are quoting from a source, use quotation marks and make sure the sentence includes the information about where you read the quote.

Protect yourself:
- Make sure to give yourself enough time to complete your assignments, that way you won't be tempted to take shortcuts.
- Keep drafts of your paper. Sometimes a student may be unfairly accused of plagiarizing. If you have copies of your notes and earlier drafts of your paper, you can prove that the thoughts are your own.

Summary

In this book we have discussed ways of finding research material.

When beginning any type of research, you must have a clear idea of the question to be answered or the problem to be solved. You begin by creating a research question. This research question will guide you through the process. The next step is to narrow or broaden your topic. Using a KWL chart and listing what you already know about your research topic and what you still need to know will determine the beginning point in the research process. After you have completed your research, you will complete the final section of the KWL chart on what you learned.

After you have decided what it is you still need to know, you may need to narrow your subject because it is too broad. If it is too broad, you will have more information than you will be able to use, making your research difficult. If you are having trouble finding any information, your topic may be too narrow, and you will have to broaden your subject question.

Finally, you will need to begin locating the sources you will use to find the answer to your research question or solution to your problem. Remember that some questions may require just a sentence of information to answer, while others may require whole books to answer. As you move through the research process, you begin to determine the amount of information needed to answer your question.

A wide variety of sources is available to locate information. Some sources are available online and provide up-to-date information on current topics. All of the sources provide different types of information and are unique as to how that information is delivered. A good researcher always verifies the facts found with information on the same topic in at least two additional sources.

One of the most serious problems with research is plagiarism. Keeping careful notes of your work is one way to avoid accidentally copying other people's ideas and words. When in doubt, it is always better to give too much credit to a source than too little.

When you first start a research project it can seem overwhelming, but with patience you can put the pieces together.

Glossary

almanac   yearly book that provides statistics, tables, and bits of information on a variety of subjects

atlas   book containing maps, tables, and charts

caption   brief description found next to a picture or other illustration that describe or identify what is pictured

cite   list a source used in writing or research

database   searchable collection of information stored electronically

Dewey decimal system   system of classifying books and other publications into subject groups using numbers

dictionary   book used to research the spelling and meaning of words

directory   Web page that contains links to selected websites on a variety of topics

electronic source   resource found on a computer or online

encyclopedia   book, often in a set of books, that contains both short and long articles on many subjects, arranged alphabetically

glossary   alphabetical list of words and their definitions found in a book

hit   successful result of an electronic search

index   alphabetical list of terms, names, and subjects that is usually located at the back of a book. An index tells the page number where information can be found on those items.

Internet   public, worldwide system of computer networks

key word   significant word used for searching for information

KWL chart   graphic organizer to help organize information about a topic

memoir   person's written memories of a personal experience significant to others

nonfiction book   book based on fact, as opposed to fiction books, which tell a created story

online   connected to or available through a computer system

online catalog   database of resources found in the library that can be accessed through a computer

periodical   magazine, newspaper, journal, or other publication published on a regular basis

plagiarism   claiming someone else's thoughts or words as your own

primary source   actual historical record, contemporary to the time period

research   act of collecting information to solve a problem or answer a question

scanning   technique used to locate specific information by quickly reading down a page looking for key words, words in bold type, or headings

search engine   Web page that uses key words to search the Internet for websites

skimming   reading technique used to determine if the material being read contains information that can answer a question

table of contents   list of the titles of chapters or sections of a book arranged in the order in which they appear in the book

transcript   written record of an event, such as a TV show

URL   abbreviation for Uniform Resource Locator, the address of a website

Find Out More

Books

Bingham, Jane. *Behind the News: Internet Freedom: Where is the Limit?* Chicago: Heinemann Library, 2007.

Career Skills Library: Research and Information Management. New York: Ferguson, 2004.

Chin, Beverly. *How to Write a Great Research Paper.* San Francisco: Jossey Bass, 2004.

Heiligman, Deborah. *The New York Public Library Kid's Guide to Research.* New York: Scholastic Reference, 1998.

Websites

www.lib.colostate.edu/teen_research/
This site from the Colorado State University provides tips for students doing research.

Check your own local library's website for services such as "ask a librarian," and other research tools.

Disclaimer

All the Internet addresses (URLs) given in this book were valid at the time of going to press. However, due to the dynamic nature of the Internet, some addresses may have changed, or sites may have changed or ceased to exist since publication. While the author and publishers regret any inconvenience this may cause readers, no responsibility for any such changes can be accepted by either the author or the publishers. It is recommended that adults supervise students on the Internet.

Further Research

The best way to learn how to research and access information is to practice. Consider using the skills discussed in this book to research some of the following topics:

The Internet
How has the Internet changed homework and research? You may take online sources for granted, but chances are that when your parents and grandparents were in school, they didn't even own a computer. Reread the section on personal interviews (p. 37), and then conduct some interviews about the Internet with people of various ages.

Plagiarism
Review the pages on plagiarism (pp. 40–41). Plagiarism doesn't just happen in school. There have been some famous cases among adults as well. Consider researching the case Harry Potter author J.K. Rowling has brought against Steve Vander Ark's plans to publish a dictionary of Harry Potter terms.

Supporting your opinion
Review the pages on opinions and research (pp. 11–13). Many newspapers have an editorial or opinion section. Look at your local newspaper, or the online version, and find an opinion piece (in print this is often found at the back of the front section of the paper). Did the writer do a good job of backing up his or her opinions? Did he or she consider the other side? Did the writer convince you?

Dewey decimal system
Review the information on the Dewey decimal system (p. 34). Who was Melvil Dewey, and why did he invent this system? What other classification systems do libraries use?

Index